THE PLACE INSIDE

First published in 2012 by
The Dedalus Press
13 Moyclare Road
Baldoyle
Dublin 13
Ireland

www.dedaluspress.com

ISBN 978 1 906614 56 0

Dedalus Press titles are represented in the UK by
Central Books, 99 Wallis Road, London E9 5LN
and in North America by Syracuse University Press, Inc.,
621 Skytop Road, Suite 110, Syracuse, New York 13244.

Cover image © Rebecca Geden

The Dedalus Press receives financial assistance from
The Arts Council / An Chomhairle Ealaíon

THE PLACE INSIDE

Matthew Geden

DEDALUS PRESS
DUBLIN, IRELAND

ACKNOWLEDGEMENTS

Acknowledgements are due to the editors of the following in which a number of these poems or versions of them originally appeared: *The Cork Literary Review, Fire, The Moth, Poetry Ireland Review, Poetry Salzburg Review, Southword* and *The Stony Thursday Book.*

CONTENTS

for Tom and Rebecca

Time Passes

after Pierre Reverdy

The first star shining in the sky is already reflected on the cabin's windowpane. The traveller, on the road too long, without a stone to sit on, without the shelter of a tree in the too-vast night with the noises coming from the distance, fled before the vague hint of fear.

He never found any shelter other than space. The light had fallen bit by bit, at the angles of the cross, at the summit of Calvary and against the ruined steps that slide into a ditch by the crossroads where the uphill road begins. He saw the bright tracks of another who had stopped there for a long time. The one who has always gone on ahead whilst you were here waiting.

Fireball

for Derek Robinson

We were peering through the dark,
which wasn't dark at all, faint
Mercury, bright Venus, constellations
and a wry crescent moon.
The Dog Star flickered
a sea-blue eye back at us,
the sky silent as unseen clouds
of ash drifted on the wind.
And slowly through spherical space
a fizzling flare, a Lyrid fireball,
dropped like volcanic rain.
You rang God who had missed
it all but told us what to expect:
continued disintegration,
sunshine and occasional showers.

Mountain Temple

after Zekkia, 1336–1405

I have closed the door on a thousand hills
To live here amidst the clouds and birds.
I spend my day watching the slopes
As keen winds infiltrate my door.
An evening meal of pine flowers,
The dyed robes of a true monk –
What dreams can the world offer
To draw me down from this dark mountain?

The Big House

after Hanshan

Accelerating past a big
                house long ruined
my restless mind is moved
                to remember its residents;
tall gates, small
                broken-down fences,
imposing gravestones, little
                ramshackle graves,
weathered shrub,
                its shadow shaking,
the endless sighs of yew trees;
                how unexceptional
were these men whose bones
                rest here – none
are mentioned
                in the great poems.

Portrait

As mysterious an existence as Lough Ine;
the surprising salt taste, the dark waters,
the strangeness that flows in on the tide.
Serious research provides a glimpse of nature:
ideas, gossip and the uniqueness of things.
You have moved through history disdainful
of the records of the few, the silence of the many.
Instead you sit for hours in the present,
a life full of everyday interest and care.
Words cannot diminish your serene standing,
the place inside the poem where you dwell
up to your ankles in a rippling rock pool,
slow smile in the differing light and deep.

Motherland

What country is this? I ask
waking from a travelling dream,
the air strange and unfamiliar faces
walking on and off a home-made stage.
No one looks at me so I stare
at their reflected world, realign
myself to the stale spittle
of disturbed sleep, disorientation.

I'm a child sent out unarmed
to fight for air; there is only
so much out there and I gasp
between the steady drops of rain.

Fragile the form held between fingers
from first to last, top to toe;
beneath this crushing weight
the world must surely crack,
and yet there is resistance
even now in the primal scream.

It's that first cigarette of the morning;
the dawn chorus hacks at the frozen
air and the dole queue shuffles
uncomfortably at each passing glance.

And then one day I think of you
and long to escape the cold,
step off the ferry and into a future
of broken-down castles,
cars rusting passively in the bush.

If you have studied the night sky
you'll have seen slight changes,
a rearrangement of atmosphere.
We live in rain and become sprites,
bare indentations on the soft bog.

There's no purity in nature;
the unbelievable in a speck
of dust or lyric of a song.
We bathe in summer's sonic
wash, beside the tumbling water
and the angels in the trees.

I belong in rootlessness,
evade the touch that isn't
there, dodge a future that can
in any case never have been.

The wind sings the treetops into
existence and reluctantly a leaf
detaches itself, falls by the wayside,
a graceful way to go astray.
It waves me forth, I'll follow it.

A Week in Eden

i POOLSIDE

A lounge lizard basks in the midday
sun, sleeps through the deals he might
have made, sweats out the stress;
a salt line inked into his brown brow.
There's a splash in the pool, sharp
intake of breath, amusement all around
at the water-shock that tingles
through the limbs. The days are precious
now; the heat on his back, loose
change in the pocket and an open book.
He dreams a sing-song voice beside him,
grazie, he murmurs; *prego*, you're welcome.

ii EDEN

Darkness inches over Eden;
street lights flicker, come on
throughout the funereal valley,
cars still flit to and fro, into
and out of the oncoming
night. Church bells toll,
ring out, a dog barks
and love lies waiting
tender and trembling beneath
the crisp white sheets of morning.

iii LEMONS

I bite the bitterness;
taste the dark plunge
into the lemon grove,

sudden loss of sunlight
and gulping, gasping
for air, fighting to

break the surface,
rising above the town,
reaching for the clouds.

iv THE ROAD TO ARCO

Alè, against the current,
into the wind, *scattante;* so much
depends on balance and poise.
You are ever-moving light,
flickering on the pathways,
rewound occasionally on the cine-
film of memory. The reel cracks,
fades over time, and yet
destined to outlast the two
in tandem, racing to the line.

v WATERLAND

Out of the rain and into the light;
bussed out across the lagoon,
we walk on water, step lightly
over the layers of a lost world.

Later I lose myself as night sinks
into dark waters, alleyways close
in around me and I can taste
the local salt on my skin.

We return to the masked world;
lights flicker and fall, rivers run
beneath us, what to make of it all?
We crawl back through a thunderstorm.

vi AT DUSK

the mountains blush
under the glint
in your eye

vii GOODBYE TO ALL THAT

This is the way to say goodbye;
love among the lizards on the river-
bank, their webbed feet run for cover,
sunlight and silence filters through the leaves.
Let's linger by the water, beneath
the mountain rock, the ample shade
of a parasol, the fizz of Prosecco,
the patient hum of the bus for home.

Limbo

*However, not only the creation, but we who have
the first fruits of the Spirit also groan inwardly as
we eagerly await our adoption, the redemption
of our bodies.*
    —Romans 8:23

Last night I acquired two ghosts
in a vial; surprised between the living
and the dead, bottled at source
and sold off like rare champagne.

I stare into their nothingness
and envy the limits of *their* world:
they are becalmed by holy water,
baptized by droplets of belief.

I can't go back, return to the house
where I was born, the spinney
in which I lived. I would see
myself in the hallway, outside
the living-room door, listening for news
of the adult world, my childhood in limbo.

Doubting Thomas

Beatific that smile crossing the possible,
raised from the dead dark earth:
steady in the sunlight a hand
reaches out. Touch, a gaping blemish
in the smooth skin. It can never
be said, what went on between
the two of us, those moments
have long passed understanding.
We might have gone to Moscow
in the Cold War, wandered
the snow-struck streets, gazed
in wonder at our lost leader.

Breath

for Eugene O'Connell

If I strain to hear the wind
I can; it breezes down unfamiliar
lanes, whispers down the chimney
as I stoke the end of summer fire,
curtains drawn against the dark.

Somewhere in the distance a car
heads home or out beyond the ghosts
the souls left wandering the ruins
of a farm, a bachelor existence
that drowned in the bottom of a glass.

I too take my medicine, try to spin
out some respite from the self-
conscious public roles played out
beneath the bright lights. Are you
on holiday? Isn't the weather grand?

I've locked the outside out, I'm
trying to close in upon the silence,
hunt it down in motionless pursuit,
one more line to go, one more
breath always just out of reach.

The Gorges of Crete

Come now. Descend between the words. Narrow strip of sky. A few moments' solitude. Glimpses of adult males are rare. Cliffs rise and the shadows engulf. All the way. Twists and turns. Catch of breath. Hold it. A chasm below and there is – there was a flourishing community. A bygone age, a silent bat. Run. Run and dive into the water.

Transformation

Stretched in the post-coital sun …
Weedy grass surrounds your resting
body, reaches for the light.

I wash the kettle in the stream,
slippery fish wriggle past, slithering
onwards, eventfully out of sight.

Cold water poured on dying embers
smoking like a cigarette, I turn
to see you flicker a lizard glance.

Warmer now, the heat is remembered –
stored inside, it might simmer for days,
a flash of the tail and you're in the shade.

Conversations

When I concentrate I can
   hear the robin,
the shrill alarm call
   of the oystercatcher.

I close my eyes and
   misremember the words,
some part of this life
   flies after the birds.

Notation

I take out my notebook
seated beneath the fig tree
reminders of fruit
                    suspended
a crescent moon
somewhere out of sight
distant traffic
and a trickle of water

      *

I find myself
thinking of tomorrow's twitter
the hyphens
the mad curlicues
of chaffinch
the sparrow
that has darted
through the hall
the coming and going
all that begins again
the brush of colour
on a weary world

      *

the institute of technology
propels the words
urges them onwards
small songs
break from the undergrowth

I have cradled
a dead tit
its blue reflection
already aloft
perfect as an eggshell
waiting to be broken
from the inside out
a pair of collared doves
like nervous ghosts
at the battlefield
peck the scattered
seed in the dirt

*

I take note
in the darkness
my eyes flicker
able to hold
the different tenses
the strain of shapes
that are and aren't there
the shadow beneath the shadow
the air tastes of ice
there is a flutter
of wings above me
the dark intent
the presence
the coldness
in the hours
before the dawn

At The Green Inn

after Rimbaud

For eight days I'd destroyed my boots
On potholes. I walked into Charleroi –
The Green Inn – and asked for bread
And butter with slices of cold ham.

Happy, I stretched out my legs beneath
The green table: I studied the naïve art
On the wallpaper, and was delighted
When a busty barmaid with a glint in her eye –

A quick kiss wouldn't frighten her away! –
Smiled as she brought my bread, butter
And cooled ham on a decorated platter,

Pink and white ham flavoured with a garlic
Clove, filling my huge tankard, the froth
Turned gold in a ray of evening sunshine.

Cúchulainn

A few of us brave the sea;
small whales warm in our blubber,
splashing through the waterline,
hardships temporarily receding.

Our future lies in the waves,
the eventual susurration shipping
away from the shore. Surfing
becomes a way of life, idle

escape into daydreams and the perfect
wave, slipping past strangers,
every word in its right place,
balance corrected by a spell-check.

In our indolence we disregard
the old man muttering stormily
in the shallows, don't even
raise an arch eyebrow when

he begins to fight the horses
of the sea, "Where did it all go
wrong?" he moans, the rest of us
complicit and silent in our treachery.

Astonishment

for Derek Mahon

He wanted to astonish Paris with an apple –
your hair backlit by religious light
a fervour recollected now in the ample
assault of Burger King electric lights.

What lies beneath the colour of things?
deliberately disjointed, an uneasy stroll –
spat-out pips and all natural objects
clamour to come in from the cold.

Selective, yet mystified by what appears,
place on view a fluttering cabbage-white –
the killing jar destroys hours, years
of evolution snuffed out in the night.

Studiously paint to discern the halo,
recover the real place in the sun,
imagine the break-downs, the fractures,
the other world present in this one.

Inheritance

for Aidan Higgins

*I was already being consumed by memories
in Mumu's womb and by her memories
prior to mine and by her granny's prior to
her, bypassing my mother, stretching as far
back as accommodating memory could
reach into the past.*
—*Donkey's Years*, Aidan Higgins

Passed on like a parcel
family faults and memories
packed tightly with string
a mass of contradictions
this unasked-for birthday present.

The sun shines because it must
provide. Words are handed
down, crafted sentences ignore
the ghost that calls, "Don't
look back. Never look back."

In the Woods

for Caroline

The stream seeps into my shoes,
soaks through my socks; my
chilled feet march independently
on and we climb to higher ground
where the sunlight brushes the branches
into life, leaves and green shoots
blister bright upon the boughs.
We amble as if lost, but drawn
irresistibly towards the top, hoping
that the higher we reach the further
we see; an iron age hill-fort
or exiled llama on the skyline.
Somehow we find our hands entwined,
ageing fingers twist and curl
into each other, stiff and deliberate
as the seasons change, the urgent
grass growing beneath our feet.
We breathe out the last of winter;
your free hand searches for
the car keys, and I think
we're not out of the woods yet.

Sigh

after Mallarmé

My soul lifts towards your forehead, calm sister,
Dreams of an autumn littered with ruddy stains,
And towards the rootless sky of your angelic eye
As though in a melancholy garden,
Faithfully, a jet of water sighs at the heavens!

Towards the tender blue of pale, pure October
Which reflects endless boredom on big pools
And on stagnant water where the browned agony
Of the leaves blows in and ploughs a cold furrow,
The yellow sun drags out in one long ray.

The Other World

To be a mist on a spring morning,
a presence in the early hours
and then to lift as a slow-motion
conjuror, disappear inland on the breeze,
reveal the light and a fading memory.

The Drop

The world shimmers in miniature;
suspended in space, refraction
changes perspective and nothing
is exactly how I remembered.
So, I retreat to my bubble
and an inner string quartet,
perfect to dispel the silence,
the tensions and unease
that stretch an elongated drop.

And when it all comes down,
bursts upon the dark impassive
earth, where will I find you
again? how will we meet?
like two lost lovers turning
back time in some imagined street?

Hotel

He pushes open the Push door,
makes his quiet way through
the foyer, past conversations,
friends and family. He tries to say
something meaningful but
there is music and laughter
and he loses the thread of what
it is to speak so presses hands
and smiles, keeps walking, right
through and out of the exit
where the cold night awaits
and the river drifts down to the sea.

Meltdown

Scratch the surface, dig a little
deeper, let the soil run through
your fingers and, down in the dirt
where only the blind can see,

lie the lives left behind, their
days darkened by this disorder
that fragments the whole, breaks
families, tears them apart.

If you could drill back through time
to the still-burning core ... a furnace
cools even now as we hurtle bravely
on, one more mathematical meltdown in store.

Travelling by Touch

Dreamlike, I trace the path
out along the headland;
the long grass almost brushes
my trailing hands, my finger-
tips altered, bloodied by the years.
I cross the soundless miles,
the wildlife scattered in the dark,
my heart racing to the familiar
notch in the coastline. X marks
the spot where my hand rests
on its midnight rendezvous.

One Last Glance

I'm on the edge, halfway out
the door, and you are further
now than you've ever been before.
My love, my pale blue dot,
I carry your songs, waves breaking
on the shore, and you are further
now than you've ever been before.

Red Wrigglers

Benevolent in a spadeful
of soil, if spared the beak
they will burrow down to earth,

disappear into the underworld,
a journey through the Neolithic
handbag, the dead red lips

kissing the new life,
wriggling back into the black
where once it all began.

Scrubland

Where nothing happens, does it?
because no one is listening
to the crackling implosion
bursting in and out of life
over time, as sunlight
drips between the leaves
and workers scuttle to and fro,
their thankless toil trampled
sporadically into the soil.
From above you can just
make out a faint impression,
is that a wall? the edge
of a long-forgotten boundary?
does it mark the place where
someone once passed over
or the way ahead? a gradual
darkening, reassuring dampness,
occasional voices breaking through?

Nature Walk

Every spring I go back, travel
into the past where the daffodils
are half my height and the woods
a pathway to a long aloneness;

dark patches of damp in the shade,
voices filter into leafy nothingness.
I try to find my way past
the barbed-wire fence; the undergrowth

tears holes in my skin, the farther
in I go the farther out I am,
looking for the house that isn't there,
the world that can't be shared.

Dark Path

for Rebecca

There are roads, old lanes,
almost lost in the landscape
where the clouds roll in and
the rain storms on from the west.

I walk ahead of you, older
shoulders braced to take the brunt,
soaking up the heavier rounds –
the sleet fired from the sky.

We are together on a dark path
struggling with the silence as the tempest
passes. Take comfort in the footprints.
Try to focus on the light.

Wulf and Eadwacer

It's as though my people were made
an offering. They'll kill him if he comes
near. Our lives are different now.
Wulf is on one land and I upon another.
Immovable rock surrounded by swamp.
They are barbarians over there:
they'll kill him if he comes near.
Our lives are different now.
How I've yearned for my wandering
Wulf, eyes streaming in the rain,
comforted in a warrior's arms,
wrapped in joy and grief together.
Wulf, my Wulf, I am lovesick,
your absence and my appetite saw
to that, I don't crave food.
Are you listening, Eadwacer? A wolf
will carry our child to the woods.
What was never joined is easily divided.
It seems our song is sung.

The Simple Life

after Horace

They say there are benefits in penury,
it's a hearty way of life. Simple fare
settles steady in the stomach, richness
sticks in the craw. Too much caviar
or oysters leave a bitter taste
and make the belly ache. Have you seen
how diners blanch when they get up
to leave? Bloated with excess, they
are lightened only by the bill.
On the other hand your man who can't
afford to eat out is fitter and faster
off the mark if he ever needs to be;
surely he'll live the better life
foregoing wealth but hale and healthy?

Mercurial

She stole my heart, vanished
into the black maw of space,
a flash of heels kicking up
the dust, dirt in my face.

I was surprised by her extremes,
the way she seared her name
on my skin, then melted
the drifting ice-caps deep inside.

Some days she turned a cold eye
on my gaze, hostile to attention,
but I'm still in thrall, spinning,
and circling like a satellite,

still hoping to bump into her
one dark night, some sunny day.

Deep Song of the South

I seek in my flesh
the traces of your lips.
        —Lorca

Still even in the song of summer,
there are silent backroads
where busyness is a faint hum,
a small nest in the background.

There are cliff-top walks
that teeter in sunlight,
golden glints in the rolls
and folds, flickers in the finite.

The moon rises
in some northern
sky, illuminates
a different time.

The easy crush of grass
pressed underfoot; soon to straighten
towards the sky, to surpass
the soft soil, lean into the wind.

Sailing-boats skim the surface
of the possible; such slow calm,
an effortless drift, a glide across
the terrible – the absent storm.

Your letter tells
me nobody eats
oranges under
the full moon.

Pale, fleshy skin lies exposed
to the fair weather. Traces of fat
burn, gently acquire a red
tinge as the sun's rays pulsate.

Something is missing from the scene,
the cormorant disappears from sight,
summer yellows the daydream
still sinks into night.

Another wanders
through shadows,
all I remember
are the lips.

Robert Louis Stevenson in Kinsale

The truth lies in perception
or the vagaries of a poet's tale
told at a long lunch between
rain-bursts as the floodwaters rise
and a darkness seeps across
the carpet. The poet is a monster,
rages against the calling of time;
punches, kicks and flails
but also charms an audience –
tells outrageous stories of the local
bar, makes his mark on the town map.
Yo ho ho and a bottle of rum!

Tom Courtenay, Philip Larkin
and the Butterfly

Am I a man who dreamt of being a butterfly,
or am I a butterfly dreaming that I am a man?
—Chuang Tzu

He is in the midst of death,
or life as some of us prefer,
when out of the air and under the light
a butterfly rises and falls onto the page
like a pause painted in the margins.
We watch as it spreads its orange wings,
a flutter of light in the darkness,
a message delivered to the gods.

Promenade

after Montale

The breeze blows harder, darkness torn asunder,
and your shadow cast upon the delicate
railing is misshapen. It's too late

for you to be yourself. Down from the palm
the mouse falls, lightning hits the touchpaper
on the fluttering eyelash of your glance.

Driving Home

after Brecht

Driving home in a brand new car,
in the rain and evening dark,
we saw a sorry sight: a man
hitching a ride, desperation in his eyes.
There was room enough and we drove
on and I said to the silence, no
we cannot carry anyone with us.
We travelled on, an hour or two,
when the tears began to fall,
shocked at the words I'd said
and the hopelessness of it all.

Tether

In the labourer's cottage
the electricity was turned
off a week ago; he lives
in a black place. A dog
barks from somewhere outside,
he gets up to fetch some rope.

Deluge

They come down from the city
in the middle of the night;
the gentle thrum of big-litre
engines propels them cross-country,

a dismal dispersal like mustard
gas blinding us in our beds.
Those of us who wake
stumble into an altered state

as though still stoned and not
impoverished as we really are.
The next day the rain begins
and our possessions simply wash away.

The Love Bats

I lie awake and think of them;
swooping, biting and sucking
their way through the night.

Their dark flutter sends shivers
through my heart. Desire
is a black nocturnal animal,

footsteps approach my door, and you
arrive in a negligee with skin exposed:
something to sink my teeth into.

The Green Man

I fold myself into the foliage;
if you look long enough you can
see me there, haunting the hedgerow,
the fire in my eyes dampened
by the end-of-summer rain.

Age is catching up with me:
my hair starting to fall out,
clumps trampled in the mud
and no green shoots sprouting
from my skin-tight skull.

I'm a figure of fun now, a foot-
note to the various mythologies
largely subsumed by the information
age or an excuse to strip
and dance naked in the dark.

There was a time of reverence,
a time I might have meant something
to someone, when branches creaked
and all of us reached upwards
growing our way to the sun.

One day, like you, I'll disappear,
sink back into the brown mulch,
slide through history in reverse,
age replaced by age and the silence
shattered by an almighty bang.

Pebble

Weary of it all we went west,
leaving behind the unpaid bills,
the begging letters we had meant
to write. Little by little
the traffic almost disappeared
and the night wrapped its arms
around us and our breathing
slowed and calmed into the quiet
of the engine smoothing our way
to the coast. We stepped outside;
worlds were shimmering in the dark,
pulses echoing through space
and, as we vanished, a far-off
star exploded, a distant pebble
cast into a dark sea.

Time to Go

after Catullus 46

Now spring rolls over into warmth
And the sky's seasonal rage
Is calmed by a welcome breeze,
Time to leave the rocky Cork coast
And the rich green fields inland.
Let's pack our bags and fly!
Thoughts drift to the continent,
Restless feet are ready to follow.
Goodbye, friends and family,
We may all leave home together
But each returns alone.